Speas Elementary School
Media Center

Title I
Winston-Salem
Forsyth County Schools

EXPLORING COUNTRIES

Lebanon

by Lisa Owings

BELLWETHER MEDIA • MINNEAPOLIS, MN

BLASTOFF! 5 READERS

Note to Librarians, Teachers, and Parents:

Blastoff! Readers are carefully developed by literacy experts and combine standards-based content with developmentally appropriate text.

Level 1 provides the most support through repetition of high-frequency words, light text, predictable sentence patterns, and strong visual support.

Level 2 offers early readers a bit more challenge through varied simple sentences, increased text load, and less repetition of high-frequency words.

Level 3 advances early-fluent readers toward fluency through increased text and concept load, less reliance on visuals, longer sentences, and more literary language.

Level 4 builds reading stamina by providing more text per page, increased use of punctuation, greater variation in sentence patterns, and increasingly challenging vocabulary.

Level 5 encourages children to move from "learning to read" to "reading to learn" by providing even more text, varied writing styles, and less familiar topics.

Whichever book is right for your reader, Blastoff! Readers are the perfect books to build confidence and encourage a love of reading that will last a lifetime!

This edition first published in 2015 by Bellwether Media, Inc.

No part of this publication may be reproduced in whole or in part without written permission of the publisher. For information regarding permission, write to Bellwether Media, Inc., Attention: Permissions Department, 5357 Penn Avenue South, Minneapolis, MN 55419.

Library of Congress Cataloging-in-Publication Data

Owings, Lisa.
  Lebanon / by Lisa Owings.
     pages cm. – (Blastoff! Readers: Exploring Countries)
  Includes bibliographical references and index.
  Summary: "Developed by literacy experts for students in grades three through seven, this book introduces young readers to the geography and culture of Lebanon"– Provided by publisher.
  Audience: Ages 7-12.
  ISBN 978-1-62617-176-3 (hardcover : alk. paper)
  1. Lebanon–Juvenile literature. I. Title.
  DS80.O86 2015
  956.92–dc23
                                                            2014034756

Printed in the United States of America, North Mankato, MN.

Contents

Where Is Lebanon?

Syria

Mediterranean
Sea

Lebanon

★
Beirut

Israel

Lebanon is a narrow country in western Asia. It covers about 4,015 square miles (10,400 square kilometers). The country lies in the **Middle East** where Asia, Africa, and Europe meet. Syria surrounds Lebanon to the north and east. Lebanon shares its southern border with Israel.

Lebanon's western coast stretches along the Mediterranean Sea. About 128 miles (206 kilometers) off the coast is the island nation of Cyprus. Lebanon's capital and largest city is Beirut. It stands on a small **peninsula** that juts out from the Mediterranean coast.

Did you know?
The name *Lebanon* comes from a word meaning "white." The country is thought to be named for its white, snow-covered mountains.

Mountain ranges **dominate** Lebanon's landscape. The rugged Lebanon Mountains run through the center of the country. The highest of their snowy peaks, Qurnat al-Sawdā', is more than 10,000 feet (3,000 meters) tall. Along the Syrian border rises the Anti-Lebanon Range.

fun fact

The Jeita Grotto is a system of caves connected by an underground river. It is the longest cave system in the Middle East. Visitors enjoy its beautiful rock formations.

Between the two mountain ranges is the Bekaa Valley. The Litani River flows south across the rich farmland there. Several shorter rivers run west from the mountains to the Mediterranean. Sandy beaches dot a narrow **plain** along the seacoast. Lebanon has mild, rainy winters. Summers are hot and dry. The weather is warmest along the coast and coolest in the mountains.

Did you know?

In 1998, Lebanon's cedar forest and the surrounding valley became protected. The area is now a UNESCO World Heritage site.

Forest of the Cedars of God

Long ago, Lebanon's mountain slopes were thick with cedar trees. The wood from these giant **evergreens** was highly valuable. It was used for building ships and places of worship. Cedars became the national **symbol** of Lebanon. Today, only a few ancient cedar **groves** remain.

The Forest of the Cedars of God grows in a valley between the highest peaks of the Lebanon Mountains. The largest of these great trees are 115 feet (35 meters) tall and 45 feet (14 meters) around. Some are more than 1,000 years old. The valley where they grow has long been considered **sacred**. Some of the first Christian **monasteries** were built there. Religious groups sought shelter and solitude in this holy place.

! fun fact
A cedar tree appears in the center of Lebanon's national flag.

jackal

Human activity has destroyed much of Lebanon's wilderness. However, many plants and animals still survive in the country. Spiky hedgehogs scurry around dry and rocky areas. Wild cats, wild boars, and jackals take shelter in forests. Rare wolves and striped hyenas prey on deer and smaller animals.

chameleon

golden eagle

hedgehog

Lebanon is also a gathering place for **migrating** birds. Falcons, buzzards, and eagles circle over the mountains and Bekaa Valley in spring. Coastal areas and marshes attract flocks of flamingos, storks, and herons. Other colorful birds also pass through on their way to and from Europe and Africa. Chameleons, turtles, and snakes can be found in many habitats. Off the coast, whales and sharks swim among schools of fish.

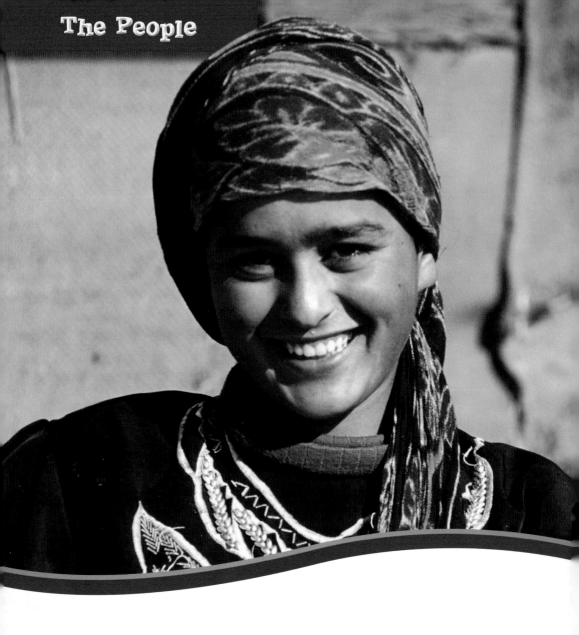

Lebanon is one of the most crowded countries in the Middle East. Nearly 6 million people share this tiny nation. More than nine out of every ten Lebanese are Arab. Their **ancestors** were originally from the Arabian Peninsula. Most of the rest of Lebanon's people are Armenian. The country is also home to Palestinians and others who fled their homes due to war.

Almost all Lebanese speak Arabic, the official language. Some also speak Armenian, English, or French. The people of Lebanon practice a variety of different religions. Just over half are Muslim. About two out of every five are Christian. Small numbers of Jews, Buddhists, and Hindus also live in Lebanon.

Speak Lebanese Arabic!

Lebanese people use Arabic script when they write. However, Arabic words can be written in English to help you read them out loud.

English	Arabic	How to say it
hello	marhaba	MAR-hah-bah
good-bye	ma'a salaama	mah-ah sah-LAH-mah
yes	na'am	nahm
no	la'	lah
please (to males)	min fadlak	min FAHD-lahk
please (to females)	min fadlik	min FAHD-lik
thank you	shukran	SHU-krahn
friend (male)	sadiiq	sah-DEEK
friend (female)	sadiiqa	sah-DEEK-ah

13

Beirut

Most Lebanese live in Beirut and other large coastal cities. Families crowd close together in concrete apartment buildings. Many have limited access to electricity and water. The government helps people in cities afford better housing. A few groups of people still live in the countryside. They have small homes on their mountain or valley farms.

The **civil war** destroyed Lebanese roads and made travel difficult. However, many roads have since been rebuilt. Streets are now jammed with cars, buses, and taxis. People take these to school, work, or to go shopping. They get what they need at large malls, shops, and open-air markets called *souks*.

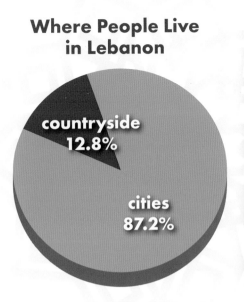

Where People Live in Lebanon

countryside 12.8%

cities 87.2%

Lebanese children start school at age 6. Most parents send their children to private schools if they can afford it. Public schools are free and have improved in recent years. Students learn to read and write in Arabic. They also learn French, English, art, and science. Many schools teach about religion.

After nine years of primary school, students take a test called the *brevet*. This helps them decide whether to study the arts or sciences in secondary school. Students can also choose to learn a specific job. If they pass the *baccalaureate* exam at the end of secondary school, they can attend one of Lebanon's many universities.

Where People Work in Lebanon

manufacturing 12%

farming 6%

services 82%

Most Lebanese earn money doing **service jobs**. Many have these types of jobs in banks, shops, or office buildings. Others serve **tourists** at local attractions or in hotels and restaurants. Some Lebanese work in factories. They make food products, clothing, jewelry, and building materials. Many of these products are shipped to other countries in the Middle East and Europe.

Farming is another important job in Lebanon. Along the coast, farmers grow vegetables and **citrus fruits**. Apples, olives, and grapes need cooler mountain air. Grains thrive in the valley. Many farmers also raise chickens, sheep, or goats.

19

Lebanon's landscape offers a wide variety of activities. Thrill-seekers ski down snowy mountain slopes in winter. In summer, hiking and mountain biking are popular. Beaches along the coast are gathering places for swimmers and sunbathers. Lebanese also enjoy boating, diving, and windsurfing.

Soccer is a favorite sport throughout the country. Some sports fans prefer basketball or volleyball. In the evenings, people like to visit friends or go to the movies. Dining out and going to dance clubs are other popular activities. A night in might involve chatting with family, playing video games, or watching TV.

fun fact

The *dabke* is Lebanon's national dance. Dancers form a line and do fancy footwork in time with catchy music.

Lebanese love to share meals with family and friends. Most meals feature several dishes, and guests are always offered plenty to eat. A spread of small dishes called *mezze* is often served for special occasions. Mezze usually includes a chickpea dip called hummus. *Tabbouleh* salads of grains and herbs are also common.

Vegetable dishes such as lentils and rice are popular. Favorite meats include lamb and chicken. *Kibbeh* is a classic dish of ground lamb or beef mixed with wheat and spices. Grilled *kebabs* can be made with any type of meat. For dessert, Lebanese enjoy fruit with clotted cream called *ashta*. *Baklava* is also popular. This flaky pastry is layered with nuts and honey or sweet syrup.

kebabs

kibbeh

fun fact

Lebanese use flatbread or lettuce to scoop up their favorite foods.

Eid al-Fitr

Did you know?

During *Eid al-Adha*, wealthy Muslims share meat with those who may be less fortunate.

New Year's

Different religious groups in Lebanon celebrate different holidays. Muslims **fast** during the holy month of Ramadan. They mark the end of Ramadan with *Eid al-Fitr*. Most people dress in new clothes. Then they visit, feast, and pray with loved ones. Families also exchange gifts.

Christian Lebanese celebrate Easter in spring. Most families attend church services and spend time with family and friends. They also feast on cakes and stuffed chicken or turkey. Winter brings Christmas along with its light displays and **Nativity scenes**. Families gather to eat a special dinner, go to church, and exchange gifts. All Lebanese celebrate national holidays. They welcome the New Year with dazzling fireworks. Independence Day on November 22 is filled with speeches and parades.

The Phoenicians were an ancient people who settled along Lebanon's coast around 3000 BCE. They soon began trading with nearby Egypt. The Phoenicians provided cedar, dyed cloth, and salt. In return, Egyptians gave them precious metals and stones. The Phoenicians' wealth and power grew as their ships carried them across the Mediterranean Sea. They ruled the area until around the 800s BCE.

fun fact
Phoenicians invented an early form of the alphabet we use today.

The **ruins** of great Phoenician cities can still be found along the Lebanese coast. Ancient temples, tombs, and **artifacts** help us understand how the Phoenicians lived. Some feature Phoenician writing. These structures are reminders of the history that shaped Lebanon into the trading center and religious **refuge** it is today.

Fast Facts About Lebanon

Lebanon's Flag

Lebanon's flag features three horizontal bands of red, white, and red. The red represents the struggle for freedom, while the white symbolizes peace and purity. In the center of the flag is a green cedar tree. The cedar tree is a biblical symbol of wealth and strength. Lebanon adopted this flag in 1943.

Official Name: Lebanese Republic

Area: 4,015 square miles (10,400 square kilometers); Lebanon is the 170th largest country in the world.

Capital City:	Beirut
Important Cities:	Tripoli, Sidon, Tyre
Population:	5,882,562 (July 2014)
Official Language:	Arabic
National Holiday:	Independence Day (November 22)
Religions:	Muslim (54%), Christian (40.5%), Druze (5.5%), very small numbers of Jews, Baha'is, Buddhists, Hindus, and Mormons
Major Industries:	services, tourism, manufacturing, farming
Natural Resources:	iron ore, limestone, sand, salt
Manufactured Products:	food products, textiles, jewelry, cement, wood products, chemicals, metals
Farm Products:	citrus fruits, grapes, olives, apples, vegetables, potatoes, poultry, sheep, goats
Unit of Money:	Lebanese pound; the pound is divided into 100 piastres.

Glossary

ancestors—relatives who lived long ago

artifacts—items made long ago by humans; artifacts tell people today about people from the past.

citrus fruits—fruits with thick skins and pulpy insides

civil war—a war between different groups within the same country

dominate—to be the main feature of something

evergreens—trees that have needle-like leaves and stay green year-round

fast—to choose not to eat

groves—small groups of trees

Middle East—a region of southwestern Asia and northern Africa; this region includes Egypt, Iran, Iraq, Israel, Lebanon, Saudi Arabia, Syria, and other nearby countries.

migrating—traveling from one place to another, often with the seasons

monasteries—places where monks live and work together; monks are part of religious communities that usually live by strict rules.

Nativity scenes—displays that show the birth of Jesus, an important figure in the Christian religion

peninsula—a section of land that extends out from a larger piece of land and is almost completely surrounded by water

plain—a large area of flat land

refuge—a place that provides shelter or protection

ruins—the physical remains of a human-made structure

sacred—holy and deserving of great respect

service jobs—jobs that perform tasks for people or businesses

symbol—something that stands for something else

tourists—people who travel to visit another place

To Learn More

AT THE LIBRARY

Fullman, Joe. *Ancient Civilizations.* New York, N.Y.: DK Publishing, 2013.

Perdew, Laura. *Understanding Lebanon Today.* Hockessin, Del.: Mitchell Lane Publishers, 2015.

Senker, Cath. *Lebanon.* Minneapolis, Minn.: Clara House Books, 2010.

ON THE WEB

Learning more about Lebanon is as easy as 1, 2, 3.

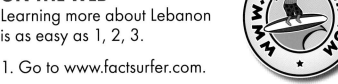

1. Go to www.factsurfer.com.

2. Enter "Lebanon" into the search box.

3. Click the "Surf" button and you will see a list of related web sites.

With factsurfer.com, finding more information is just a click away.

Index

The images in this book are reproduced through the courtesy of: ramzihachicho, front cover; Anton Petrus, pp. 6-7; Hussein Malla/ AP Images, pp. 7, 24; jcarillet/ Getty Images, pp. 8-9; mooinblack, pp. 10-11; Tom Linster, p. 11 (top); Michal Ninger, p. 11 (center); Martin Sevcik, p. 11 (bottom); Guido Alberto Rossi/ Glow Images, p. 12; Robert Harding Picture Library/ SuperStock, p. 14; dinosmichail, p. 15; Marway Naamani/ Getty Images, pp. 16-17; Christian Kober/ Glow Images, p. 18; Anwar Amro/ Stringer/ Getty Images, p. 18 (left); M Itani/ Alamy, p. 19 (right); Stefan Auth/ Glow Images, p. 20; ZUMA Press, Inc./ Alamy, p. 21; Hans Neleman/ Getty Images, p. 22; Paul Cowan, p. 23 (left); Paul Brighton, p. 23 (right); Nabil Mounzer/ EPA/ Newscom, p. 25; f8grapher, pp. 26-27; David McLain/ Getty Images, p. 27; Oleg_Mit, p. 29 (top); Asaf Eliason, p. 29 (bottom).